Complete
String Quartets

Peter Ilyitch Tchaikovsky
and
Alexander Borodin

DOVER PUBLICATIONS INC.

NEW YORK

Copyright

Published in Canada by General Publishing Company, Ltd., 30 Lesmill Road, Don Mills, Toronto, Ontario.

Published in the United Kingdom by Constable and Company, Ltd., 3 The Lanchesters, 162–164 Fulham Palace Road, London W6 9ER.

Bibliographical Note

This Dover edition, first published in 1994, is a new compilation of five scores originally published in three separate editions. Peter Ilyitch Tchaikovsky's *String Quartets Nos. 1–3* were originally published in a single volume (including an unfinished *String Quartet in B-flat Major*) in an authoritative Russian edition, n.d. Alexander Borodin's *Streichquartett Nr. 1* was originally published by M. P. Belaieff, Frankfurt, n.d.; his *String Quartet No. 2* was originally published in an unidentified edition, n.d.

The Dover edition adds a unified table of contents, both reset and newly added movement headings, English translations of the original Russian footnotes in the Tchaikovsky scores, and background information about Beethoven references in Borodin's *String Quartet No. 1*. The new English footnotes have been lightly edited for easier reference to the music, and the footnote marker on p. 22 has been shifted to m. 57 for clarity.

Library of Congress Cataloging-in-Publication Data

Complete string quartets / Peter Ilyitch Tchaikovsky and Alexander Borodin.
   1 score

   Contents: No. 1 in D major, op. 11 (1871); No. 2 in F major, op. 22 (1874); No. 3 in E-flat minor, op. 30 (1875?) / Peter Ilyitch Tchaikovsky—No. 1 in A major (1877–8); No. 2 in D major (1880?) / Alexander Borodin.

   1. String quartets—Scores. I. Tchaikovsky, Peter Ilich, 1840–1893. Quartets, strings. II. Borodin, Aleksandr Porfir'evich, 1833–1887. Quartets, strings, no. 1, A major. III. Borodin, Aleksandr Porfir'evich, 1833–1887. Quartets, strings, no. 2, D major.

M452.C73   1994   94-27713
ISBN 0-486-28333-X   CIP
                                                      M

Manufactured in the United States of America
Dover Publications, Inc., 31 East 2nd Street, Mineola, N.Y. 11501

CONTENTS

Peter Ilyitch Tchaikovsky

String Quartet No. 1 in D Major

OP. 11 (1871)

(Dedicated to Sergey A. Rachinsky)

I.

1) m. 23, Vln. I: In the parts edition checked by the composer (1889), the last 8th reads:

2) mm. 29–33, Cello: In the parts edition checked by the composer (1889), this passage reads:

mf largamente e cantabile

4   Tchaikovsky, *String Quartet No. 1* (I)

1) m. 65, Vla.: The manuscript and printed score (1872) have an *mp*; apparently the composer used that nuance to call attention to the transfer of the melody from Vln. II to Vla.

1) mm. 86–100, Cello: In the printed parts checked by the composer (1889), the passage reads:

1) m. 100, Cello: In the parts edition checked by the composer (1889), this part of the measure is notated: Possibly this is more correct.

1) mm. 134–138, Cello: In the parts edition checked by the composer (1889) this passage reads:

1) Poco accelerando

sempre accel.

1) m. 172, ensemble: The *ff* occurs in the parts edition checked by the composer (1889).

II.

Andante cantabile

III. Scherzo

Allegro non tanto e con fuoco

1) m. 42, Vln. II: In the parts edition checked by the composer (1889), the measure begins:

1) m. 57, ensemble: The Italian instructions occur in the parts edition checked by the composer (1889).

IV. Finale

25

1) mm. 51–52, ensemble: In the printed score (1872), Vln. I is marked *sff* and Vln. II and Cello are marked *mf*. Corrected here by analogy with mm. 254–255.

1) m. 122, ensemble: "très sec" is added here by analogy with m. 325.

Peter Ilyitch Tchaikovsky

String Quartet No. 2 in F Major
OP. 22 (1874)

(Dedicated to Grand Duke Konstantin Nikolayevich)

I.

1) m. 19, tempo: In the printed parts (1875), "quasi andantino" is added.

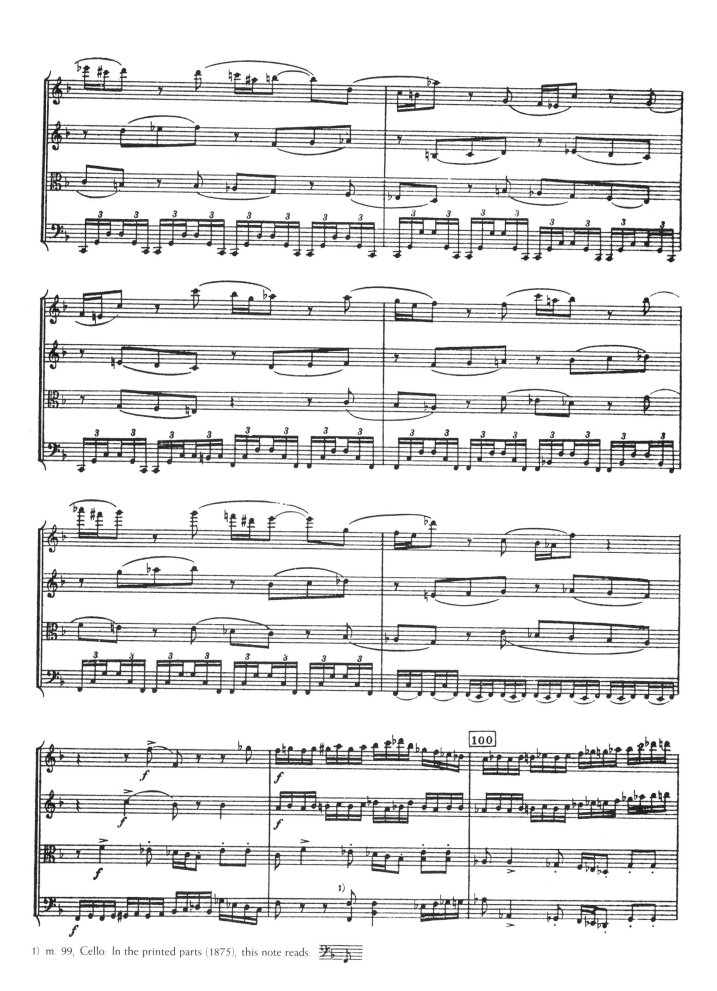

1) m. 99, Cello: In the printed parts (1875), this note reads:

1) m. 113, Cello: In the printed parts (1875), this note reads:

1) m. 131, Vla.: In the corresponding place in m. 26, the first 8th is A. There is no basis for making the two readings conform.

1) mm. 152–153, Vln. I: In the manuscript score, the passage reads:
The bowing is altered here by analogy with mm. 45–46.

1) m. 164, Cello: It is possible that the first half of this measure, by analogy with the exposition (see m. 57), should be:

II. Scherzo

1) m. 55, Vln. I: In the manuscript and printed score (1876), Vln. I is marked "riten.," the sense of which is unclear. Possibly this *ritenuto* applies only to the first three 8ths of the measure.

1) m. 271—end, Vln. I & Vla.: In the manuscript and printed score, the articulation dots are lacking.

III.

1) mm. 86–89, Cello: In the manuscript, this passage is notated in triplets: ⟨music example⟩ etc.

1) mm. 100–102, Cello: In the printed score (1876), this passage is notated: ![notation](etc.) etc.; however, in the 1875 edition,

checked by the composer, these measures are notated differently. In the present edition, this notation is carried over into the score.

1) m. 164, Vla.: In the manuscript, the second quarter is written:

IV. Finale

1) mm. 20–21, Cello: In the manuscript and printed score (1876), the passage reads: ♪ ♪ This is obviously an error.

1) m. 182, ensemble: In the manuscript and printed score (1876), the *f* occurs only in Vln. I and one measure later. This is obviously an error.

2) m. 186, Vla.: In the manuscript and printed score (1876), the *B* at the very end of the measure is marked with a ♮. Possibly this is an error and there should be a ♭ instead.

1) m. 203, Cello: In the first edition, the *E* at the very end of the measure is marked with a ♮, but in the manuscript and printed score (1876) the ♮ is lacking.

Peter Ilyitch Tchaikovsky

String Quartet No. 3 in E-flat Minor
OP. 30 (1875?)

(Dedicated to the memory of Ferdinand Laub)

I.

1) m. 255, Vla.: It is possible that a ♯ was omitted in front of the note *A*.

1) m. 469, Cello: This ♭ is suggested by analogy with m. 172, where in a completely identical place the Vla. has: Possibly the absence of the ♭ in the manuscript is an error.

1) mm. 591–559, ensemble: In the manuscript and printed score (1876), this chord here and everywhere afterward is notated as:

This notation has been changed by analogy with mm. 21 and following.

II.

Allegretto vivo e scherzando (♩=96)

1) mm. 40–41, Vln. I: In the manuscript, there are *two* tied notes across the bar line:

III.

Andante funebre e doloroso, ma con moto ($\quarternote = 56$)

IV. Finale

1) m. 177, Vln. II: Possibly the double stop 𝄞 is an error, and really should be 𝄞

Alexander Borodin

String Quartet No. 1 in A Major
"On a Theme of Beethoven"*
(1877–8)
(Dedicated to Mme. N. Rimsky-Korsakow)

*Elements of Movements I, II and IV are based on the Finale of Beethoven's *String Quartet No. 13* in B-flat Major, Op. 130.

I.

un poco meno mosso

II.

Andante con moto ♩=72

più vivo, animato ed appassionato

a tempo

Fugato
Un poco più mosso

III. Scherzo

166

Scherzo da Capo al Fine

Più animato

Flag.

45

Alexander Borodin

String Quartet No. 2 in D Major
(1880?)

(Dedicated to Ekaterina Borodin*)

*Borodin's wife; in the Belaieff edition, written "Frau Katherina Borodin."

I.

II. Scherzo

III. Notturno

IV. Finale

THE END